Keto Diet Cookbook After 50

The Best Recipes to Lose Weight, Boost Metabolism and Live Longer

Aliza Ballard

Copyright © 2021

All rights reserved.

CONTENTS

BREAKFAST 10

Coconut Gruyere Biscuits 11

Feta & Spinach Frittata with Tomatoes 15

Coconut Almond Muffins 19

Almond Butter Shake 21

Raspberry Mini Tarts 22

Morning Beef Patties with Lemon 26

Coconut Blini with Berry Drizzle 28

Pesto Bread Twists 30

Broccoli Hash Browns 32

Spinach & Fontina Cheese Nest Bites 34

LUNCH & DINNER 36

Primavera Spaghetti Squash 38

American Cobb Egg Salad in Lettuce 40

Tofu & Spinach Zucchini Lasagna 42

Roasted Stuffed Lamb Leg with Pine Nuts 44

Strawberry & Spinach Blue Cheese Salad 46

Bacon & Chicken Ranch Pizza 48

Minty Lamb with Butter Sauce 50

Feta Bacon Green Salad 52

Spinach, Kale & Mushroom Biryani 54

Seitan Kabobs with BBQ Sauce 57

Grilled Lamb Chops with Minty Sauce 59

Grana Padano Roasted Cabbage 61

Pancetta Mashed Cauliflower 62

Pancetta Wrapped Chicken Rolls 64

Fish Taco Green Bowl with Red Cabbage 65

Herbed Veal Rack 67

Cheese Scallops with Chorizo 69

Chicken Ham & Turnip Pasta 70

Kale & Mushroom Galette 71

Braised Sage-Flavored Lamb Chops 74

Turnip Chips with Avocado Dip 75

SNACK & SIDES 77

Jalapeño Nacho Wings 78

Cheesy Bacon & Eggplant Gratin 80

Wrapped Halloumi in Bacon 82

Sweet Mustard Mini Sausages 84

Chili Broccoli & Pancetta Roast 85

Chili Turnip Fries 86

Buttery Radish & Minute Steak Sauté 87

Cheddar Bacon & Celeriac Bake 88

Chicken Ham with Mini Bell Peppers 90

Crispy Baked Cheese Asparagus 92

Easy Bacon & Cheese Balls 94

DESSERTS 95

Lemon-Yogurt Mousse 96

Strawberry Chocolate Mousse 97

Maple Lemon Cake 98

Saffron & Cardamom Coconut Bars 100

Granny Smith Apple Tart 102

Chocolate Mocha Ice Bombs 104

Almond & Coconut Bark 105

Coconut Butter Ice Cream 106

Chia Pudding 107

Mom's Walnut Cookies 108

Almond Ice Cream 109

BREAKFAST

Coconut Gruyere Biscuits

Ingredients for 4 servings

- ☐ 4 eggs
- ☐ ¼ cup butter melted
- ☐ ¼ tsp salt
- ☐ 1/3 cup coconut flour
- ☐ ¼ cup coconut flakes
- ☐ ½ tsp xanthan gum
- ☐ ¼ tsp baking powder
- ☐ 2 tsp garlic powder
- ☐ ¼ tsp onion powder
- ☐ ½ cup grated Gruyere cheese

Instructions - Total Time: around 30 minutes

Preheat oven to 350 F. Line a baking sheet with parchment paper. In a food
processor, mix eggs, butter, and salt until smooth. Add coconut flour, coconut
flakes, xanthan gum, baking, garlic, and onion powders, and Gruyere cheese.

Combine smoothly. Mold 12 balls out of the mixture and arrange on the

baking sheet at 2-inch intervals. Bake for 25 minutes or until the biscuits are

golden brown.

Per serving: Cal 267; Net Carbs 5.1g, Fat 26g, Protein 12g

Feta & Spinach Frittata with Tomatoes

Ingredients for 4 servings

- ☐ 5 oz spinach
- ☐ 8 oz feta cheese, crumbled
- ☐ 1 pint cherry tomatoes, halved
- ☐ 10 eggs
- ☐ 2 tbsp olive oil
- ☐ 4 scallions, diced

Instructions - Total Time: around 35 minutes

Preheat oven to 350 F. Drizzle the oil in a casserole and place in the oven
until heated. In a bowl, whisk eggs along with pepper and salt. Stir in
spinach, feta cheese, and scallions. Pour the mixture into the casserole, top
with the cherry tomatoes and place back in the oven. Bake for 25 minutes.
Cut the frittata into wedges and serve with salad.

Coconut Almond Muffins

Ingredients for 4 servings

- ☐ 2 cups almond flour
- ☐ 2 tsp baking powder
- ☐ 8 oz ricotta cheese, softened
- ☐ ¼ cup butter, melted
- ☐ 1 egg
- ☐ 1 cup coconut milk

Instructions - Total Time: around 30 minutes

Preheat oven to 400 F. Grease a muffin tray with cooking spray. Mix flour,
baking powder, and salt in a bowl.
In a separate bowl, beat ricotta cheese and butter using a hand mixer and
whisk in the egg and coconut milk. Fold in almond flour and spoon the batter
into the muffin cups two-thirds way up. Bake for 20 minutes, remove to a
wire rack to cool slightly for 5 minutes before serving.

Almond Butter Shake

Ingredients for 2 servings

- ☐ 3 cups almond milk
- ☐ 3 tbsp almond butter
- ☐ ⅛ tsp almond extract
- ☐ 1 tsp cinnamon
- ☐ 4 tbsp flax meal
- ☐ 1 scoop collagen peptides
- ☐ A pinch of salt
- ☐ 15 drops stevia

Instructions - Total Time: around 2 minutes

Add milk, butter, flax meal, almond extract, collagen, salt, and stevia to the
blender. Blitz until uniform and smooth. Serve into smoothie glasses,
sprinkled with cinnamon.

Per serving: Cal 326; Net Carbs 6g; Fat 27g; Protein 19g

Raspberry Mini Tarts

Ingredients for 4 servings

For the crust:

- ☐ 6 tbsp butter, melted
- ☐ 2 cups almond flour
- ☐ 1/3 cup xylitol
- ☐ 1 tsp cinnamon powder

For the filling:

- ☐ 3 cups raspberries, mashed
- ☐ ½ tsp fresh lemon juice
- ☐ ¼ cup butter, melted
- ☐ ½ tsp cinnamon powder
- ☐ ¼ cup xylitol sweetener

Instructions - Total Time: around 25 min + chilling time

Preheat oven to 350 F. Lightly grease 4 mini tart tins with cooking spray. In a
food processor, blend butter, almond flour, xylitol, and cinnamon. Divide the
dough between the tart tins and bake for 15 minutes. In a bowl, mix

raspberries, lemon juice, butter, cinnamon, and xylitol. Pour filling into the
crust, gently tap on a flat surface to release air bubbles and refrigerate for 1
hour. Serve.

Per serving: Cal 435; Net Carbs 4.8g, Fat 29g, Protein 2g

Morning Beef Patties with Lemon

Ingredients for 6 servings

- ☐ 6 ground beef patties
- ☐ 4 tbsp olive oil
- ☐ 2 ripe avocados, pitted
- ☐ 2 tsp fresh lemon juice
- ☐ 6 fresh eggs
- ☐ Red pepper flakes to garnish

Instructions - Total Time: around 25 minutes

In a skillet, warm oil and fry patties for 8 minutes. Remove to a plate. Spoon avocado into a bowl, mash with the lemon juice, and season with salt and pepper. Spread the mash on the patties. Boil 3 cups of water in a pan over high heat and reduce to simmer (don't boil). Crack an egg into a bowl and put it in the simmering water. Poach for 2-3 minutes. Remove to a plate. Repeat with the remaining eggs.

Top patties with eggs and sprinkle with chili flakes.

Per serving: Cal 378; Net Carbs 5g; Fat 23g; Protein 16g

Coconut Blini with Berry Drizzle

Ingredients for 6 servings

Pancakes

- 1 cup cream cheese
- 1 cup coconut flour
- 1 tsp salt
- 2 tsp xylitol
- 1 tsp baking soda
- 1 tsp baking powder
- 1 ½ cups coconut milk
- 1 tsp vanilla extract
- 6 large eggs
- ¼ cup olive oil

Blackberry Sauce

3 cups fresh blackberries

1 lemon, juiced

½ cup xylitol

½ tsp arrowroot starch

A pinch of salt

Instructions - Total Time: around 40 minutes

Put coconut flour, salt, xylitol, baking soda and powder in a bowl and whisk
to combine. Add in milk, cream cheese, vanilla, eggs, and olive oil and whisk
until smooth. Set a pan and pour in a small ladle of batter. Cook on one side
for 2 minutes, flip, and cook for 2 minutes. Transfer to a plate and repeat the
cooking process until the batter is exhausted. Pour the berries and half cup of
water into a saucepan and bring to a boil. Simmer for 12 minutes. Pour in
xylitol, stir, and continue cooking for 5 minutes. Stir in salt and lemon juice.
Mix arrowroot starch with 1 tbsp of water; pour the mixture into the berries.
Stir and continue cooking the sauce until it thickens. Serve.

Per serving: Cal 433; Net Carbs 4.9g; Fat 39g; Protein 8.2g

Pesto Bread Twists

Ingredients for 6 servings

- ☐ 1 tbsp flax seed powder + 3 tbsp water
- ☐ 1½ cups grated mozzarella
- ☐ 4 tbsp coconut flour
- ☐ ½ cup almond flour
- ☐ 1 tsp baking powder
- ☐ 5 tbsp butter
- ☐ 2 oz pesto

Instructions - Total Time: around 35 minutes

For flax egg, mix flax seed powder with water in a bowl, and let to soak for 5
minutes. Preheat oven to 350 F. Line a baking sheet with parchment paper. In
a bowl, combine coconut flour, almond flour, and baking powder. Melt butter
and cheese in a skillet and stir in the flax egg. Mix in flour mixture until a
firm dough forms. Divide the mixture between 2 parchment papers, then use

a rolling pin to flatten out the dough of about an inch's thickness. Remove the
parchment paper on top and spread pesto all over the dough. Cut the dough
into strips, twist each piece, and place on the baking sheet. Brush with olive
oil and bake for 15-20 minutes until golden brown.

Per serving: Cal 206; Net Carbs 3g; Fat 17g; Protein 8g

Broccoli Hash Browns

Ingredients for 4 servings

- ☐ 3 tbsp flax seed powder + 9 tbsp water
- ☐ 1 head broccoli, rinsed and cut into florets
- ☐ ½ white onion, grated
- ☐ 5 tbsp vegan butter

Instructions - Total Time: around 35 minutes

In a bowl, mix flax seed powder with water and allow soaking for 5 minutes.

Pour broccoli into a food processor and pulse until smoothly grated. Transfer

to a bowl, add in flax egg and onion. Mix and let sit for 10 minutes to firm up

a bit. Melt butter in a skillet. Ladle scoops of the broccoli mixture into the

skillet, flatten and fry until golden brown, 8 minutes, turning once. Transfer

the hash browns to a plate and repeat the frying process for the remaining

broccoli mixture. Serve warm.

Spinach & Fontina Cheese Nest Bites

Ingredients for 4 servings

- ☐ 4 tbsp shredded Pecorino Romano cheese
- ☐ 2 tbsp shredded fontina
- ☐ 1 tbsp olive oil
- ☐ 1 clove garlic, grated
- ☐ ½ lb spinach, chopped
- ☐ 4 eggs
- ☐ Salt and black pepper to taste

Instructions - Total Time: around 40 minutes

Preheat oven to 350 F. Warm oil in a skillet, add garlic, and sauté for 2

minutes. Add in spinach to wilt about 5 minutes and season with salt and

pepper. Stir in 2 tbsp of Pecorino Romano cheese and fontina cheese and

remove from the heat. Allow cooling. Mold 4 (firm separate) spinach nests

on a greased sheet and crack an egg into each nest. Sprinkle with the
remaining Pecorino Romano cheese. Bake for 15 minutes. Serve right away.

Per serving: Cal 230; Net Carbs 4g; Fat 17.5g; Protein 12g

LUNCH & DINNER

Primavera Spaghetti Squash

Ingredients for 4 servings

- ☐ 1 tbsp butter
- ☐ 1 cup cherry tomatoes
- ☐ 2 tbsp parsley
- ☐ 4 bacon slices
- ☐ ¼ cup Parmesan cheese
- ☐ 3 tbsp scallions, chopped
- ☐ 1 cup sugar snap peas
- ☐ 1 tsp lemon zest
- ☐ 2 cups cooked spaghetti squash
- ☐ Salt and black pepper to taste

Instructions - Total Time: around 15 minutes

Melt the butter in a saucepan and cook bacon until crispy. Add the tomatoes
and peas, and cook for 5 more minutes. Stir in parsley, zest, and scallions and
remove the pan from heat. Stir in spaghetti and Parmesan cheese. Serve.

American Cobb Egg Salad in Lettuce Wraps

Ingredients for 4 servings

- ☐ 2 chicken breasts, cubed
- ☐ 1 tbsp olive oil
- ☐ 6 large eggs
- ☐ 2 tomatoes, seeded, chopped
- ☐ 6 tbsp cream cheese
- ☐ 1 head lettuce, leaves separated

Instructions - Total Time: around 30 minutes

Preheat oven to 400 F. Put the chicken in a bowl and coat with the olive oil.

Transfer to a greased baking sheet. Bake for 8 minutes, turning once. Bring

eggs to a boil in salted water for 10 minutes. Run the eggs in cold water, peel,

and chop into small pieces. Place them in a salad bowl. Add in the baked chicken, tomatoes, and cream cheese and mix evenly. Lay 2 lettuce leaves each as cups and fill with 2 tbsp of egg salad each. Serve.

Per serving: Cal 325; Net Carbs 4g; Fat 24.5g; Protein 21g

Tofu & Spinach Zucchini Lasagna

Ingredients for 4 servings

- ☐ 2 zucchinis, sliced
- ☐ Salt and black pepper to taste
- ☐ 2 cups cream cheese
- ☐ 2 cups tofu cheese, shredded
- ☐ 3 cups tomato sauce
- ☐ 1 cup packed baby spinach

Instructions - Total Time: around 60 minutes

Preheat oven to 370 F. Mix cream cheese, tofu, salt, and black pepper to
evenly combine. Spread ¼ cup of the mixture in the bottom of a greased
baking dish.
Lay a third of the zucchini slices on top, spread 1 cup of tomato sauce over,
and scatter one-third cup of spinach on top. Repeat the layering process two
more times to exhaust the ingredients while making sure to finish with the

last ¼ cup of cheese mixture. Grease one end of foil with cooking spray and

cover the baking dish with the foil. Bake for 35 minutes, remove foil, and

bake further for 10 minutes. Let sit for 5 minutes, make slices, and serve.

Per serving: Cal 390; Net Carbs 2g; Fat 39g; Protein 7g

Roasted Stuffed Lamb Leg with Pine Nuts

Ingredients for 4 servings

- ☐ 1 lb rolled lamb leg, boneless
- ☐ 1 ½ cups rosemary, chopped
- ☐ 5 tbsp pine nuts, chopped
- ☐ ½ cup green olives, chopped
- ☐ 3 cloves garlic, minced
- ☐ Salt and black pepper to taste

Instructions - Total Time: around 1 hour 10 minutes

Preheat oven to 400 F. In a bowl, combine rosemary, pine nuts, olives, and garlic. Season with salt and pepper. Untie the lamb flat onto a chopping board, rub rosemary mixture all over the meat. Roll lamb over the spices and tie it together using 4 strings of butcher's twine. Place lamb on a baking dish bake for 10 minutes. Cook for 40 minutes. Transfer to a clean chopping board; let it rest for 10 minutes before slicing. Serve.

Per serving: Cal 547; Net Carbs 2.2g Fat 38g; Protein 43g

Strawberry & Spinach Blue Cheese Salad

Ingredients for 2 servings

- ☐ 1 ½ cups gorgonzola cheese
- ☐ 4 cups spinach
- ☐ 4 strawberries, sliced
- ☐ ½ cup flaked almonds
- ☐ 4 tbsp raspberry vinaigrette

Instructions - Total Time: around 20 minutes

Preheat oven to 400 F. Crumble gorgonzola cheese onto 2 pieces of
parchment paper. Bake for 10 minutes. In 2 identical bowls, set them upside
down, and put 2 parchment papers on top to give the cheese a bowl-like
shape. Cool for 15 minutes. Share spinach among the bowls and drizzle with
vinaigrette. Top with almonds and strawberries.

Per serving: Cal 445; Net Carbs: 5g; Fat: 34g; Protein: 33g

Bacon & Chicken Ranch Pizza

Ingredients for 4 servings

- ☐ 3 cups shredded mozzarella
- ☐ 3 tbsp cream cheese, softened
- ☐ ¾ cup almond flour
- ☐ 2 tbsp almond meal
- ☐ 1 tbsp butter
- ☐ ¼ cup half and half
- ☐ 1 tbsp dry Ranch seasoning
- ☐ 3 bacon slices, chopped
- ☐ 2 chicken breasts
- ☐ 6 fresh basil leaves

Instructions - Total Time: around 45 minutes

Preheat oven to 390 F. Line a pizza pan with parchment paper. Microwave 2
cups of mozzarella cheese and 2 tbsp of the cream cheese for 30 seconds.

Mix in almond flour and almond meal. Spread the "dough" on the pan and bake for 15 minutes. In a bowl, mix butter, remaining cream cheese, half and half, and ranch mix; set aside. Heat a grill pan and cook the bacon for 5 minutes; set aside. Grill the chicken in the pan on both sides for 10 minutes.

Remove to a plate, allow cooling and cut into thin slices. Spread the ranch sauce on the pizza crust, followed by the chicken and bacon, and then, the remaining mozzarella cheese and basil. Bake for 5 minutes. Serve sliced.

Per serving: Cal 528; Net Carbs 4g; Fats 28g; Protein 62g

Minty Lamb with Butter Sauce

Ingredients for 4 servings

- 1 ¼ pounds rack of lamb
- 3 cloves garlic, minced
- 3 oz butter, melted
- 3 oz red wine
- A handful of mint, chopped

Butter Sauce

- 1 cup vegetable broth
- 2 tbsp olive oil
- 1 zucchini, chopped
- 2 cloves garlic, minced
- 2 oz butter
- Salt and white pepper to taste

Instructions - Total Time: around 25 min + cooling time

In a bowl, mix melted butter with red wine, salt, and 3 garlic cloves and
brush the mixture all over the lamb. Drop the chopped mint on, cover the

bowl with plastic wrap, and refrigerate to marinate. Preheat grill to 435 F and
cook the lamb for 6 minutes on both sides. Remove and let rest for 4 minutes.
Heat olive oil in a pan and sauté 2 garlic cloves and zucchini for 5 minutes.
Pour in vegetable broth and continue cooking until the liquid reduces by half,
10 minutes. Add in 2 oz of butter, salt, and pepper. Stir to melt the butter and
turn the heat off. Puree the ingredients in a food processor until smooth and
strain the sauce through a fine-mesh into a bowl. Slice the lamb, pour the
sauce over, and serve.

Per serving: Cal 553; Net Carbs 2.3g; Fat 47g; Protein 30g

Feta Bacon Green Salad

Ingredients for 4 servings

- ☐ 2 (8 oz) pack mixed salad greens
- ☐ 1 ½ cups feta cheese, crumbled
- ☐ 8 strips bacon
- ☐ 1 tbsp white wine vinegar
- ☐ 3 tbsp extra virgin olive oil
- ☐ Salt and black pepper to taste

Instructions - Total Time: around 20 minutes

Pour the salad greens in a salad bowl; set aside. Fry bacon strips in a skillet

for 6 minutes, until browned and crispy. Chop it and scatter over the salad.

Add in half of the feta cheese, toss and set aside. In a small bowl, whisk

white wine vinegar, olive oil, salt, and black pepper until well combined.

Drizzle dressing over the salad, toss, and top with the remaining cheese.

Serve.

Spinach, Kale & Mushroom Biryani

Ingredients for 4 servings

- ☐ 1 cup sliced cremini mushrooms
- ☐ 6 cups cauli rice
- ☐ Salt and black pepper to taste
- ☐ 3 tbsp ghee
- ☐ 3 white onions, chopped
- ☐ 6 garlic cloves, minced
- ☐ 1 tsp ginger puree
- ☐ 1 tbsp turmeric powder
- ☐ 2 cups chopped tomatoes
- ☐ 1 habanero pepper, minced
- ☐ 1 tbsp tomato puree
- ☐ 1 cup diced paneer cheese
- ☐ ½ cup spinach, chopped
- ☐ ½ cup kale, chopped
- ☐ ¼ cup chopped parsley
- ☐ 1 cup Greek yogurt
- ☐ 2 tbsp olive oil

Instructions - Total Time: around 1 hour 20 minutes

Preheat oven to 400 F. Microwave cauli rice for 1 minute. Remove and

season with salt and black pepper; set aside.Melt ghee in a pan over medium

heat and sauté onions, garlic, ginger puree, and turmeric.

Cook for 15 minutes, stirring regularly. Add in tomatoes, habanero pepper,

and tomato puree; cook for 5 minutes. Stir in mushrooms, paneer cheese,

spinach, kale, and 1/3 cup water and simmer for 15 minutes or until the

mushrooms soften.

Turn the heat off and stir in yogurt. Spoon half of the stew into a bowl.

Sprinkle half of the parsley over the stew in the pan, half of the cauli rice, and

dust with turmeric. Repeat the layering a second time including the reserved stew. Drizzle with olive oil and bake for 25 minutes. Serve.

Per serving: Cal 346; Net Carbs 2g; Fat 21.4g; Protein 16g

Seitan Kabobs with BBQ Sauce

Ingredients for 4 servings

- ☐ 10 oz seitan, cut into chunks
- ☐ 2 cups water
- ☐ 1 red onion, cut into chunks
- ☐ 1 red bell pepper, cut chunks
- ☐ 1 yellow bell pepper, chopped
- ☐ 2 tbsp olive oil
- ☐ 1 cup barbecue sauce
- ☐ Salt and black pepper to taste

Instructions - Total Time: around 30 min + marinating time

Bring water to a boil in a pot over medium heat, turn the heat off, and add seitan. Cover the pot and let the tempeh steam for 5 minutes; drain. Pour barbecue sauce in a bowl, add in the seitan, and toss to coat. Cover the bowl and marinate in the fridge for 2 hours. Preheat grill to 350 F. Thread the seitan, yellow bell pepper, red bell pepper,

and onion. Brush the grate of the grill with olive oil, place the skewers on it,
and brush with barbecue sauce. Cook the kabobs for 3 minutes on each side
while rotating and brushing with more barbecue sauce. Serve.

Per serving: Cal 228; Net Carbs 3.6g; Fat 15g; Protein 13g

Grilled Lamb Chops with Minty Sauce

Ingredients for 4 servings

- ☐ 8 lamb chops
- ☐ 2 tbsp favorite spice mix
- ☐ ¼ cup olive oil
- ☐ 1 tsp red pepper flakes
- ☐ 2 tbsp lemon juice
- ☐ 2 tbsp fresh mint
- ☐ 3 garlic cloves, pressed
- ☐ 2 tbsp lemon zest
- ☐ ¼ cup parsley
- ☐ ½ tsp smoked paprika

Instructions - Total Time: around 25 minutes

Preheat grill to medium heat. Rub the lamb with oil and sprinkle with spices.

Grill for 3 minutes per side. Whisk together the remaining oil, lemon juice and zest, mint, garlic, parsley, and paprika. Serve the chops with sauce.

Per serving: Cal 392; Net Carbs 0g; Fat 31g; Protein 29g

Grana Padano Roasted Cabbage

Ingredients for 4 servings

- 1 head green cabbage
- 4 tbsp melted butter
- 1 tsp garlic powder
- Salt and black pepper to taste
- 1 cup grated Grana Padano
- 1 tbsp parsley, chopped

Instructions - Total Time: around 30 minutes

Preheat oven to 400 F. Line a baking sheet with foil. Cut cabbage into
wedges. Mix butter, garlic, salt, and pepper in a bowl. Brush the mixture on
all sides of the wedges and sprinkle with some of Grana Padano cheese. Bake
for 20 minutes. Sprinkle with remaining cheese and parsley.

Per serving: Cal 268; Net Carbs 4g; Fat 19g; Protein 17.5g

Pancetta Mashed Cauliflower

Ingredients for 4 servings

- ☐ 1 head cauliflower, leaves removed
- ☐ 6 slices pancetta
- ☐ 2 cups water
- ☐ 2 tbsp melted butter
- ☐ ½ cup buttermilk
- ☐ ¼ cup Colby cheese, grated
- ☐ 2 tbsp chopped chives

Instructions - Total Time: around 40 minutes

Preheat oven to 350 F. Fry pancetta in a skillet over medium heat for 5
minutes. Let cool and crumble. Keep the pancetta fat. Boil cauli head in water
in a pot for 7 minutes. Drain and put in a bowl. Add in butter and buttermilk
and puree until smooth and creamy. Grease a casserole with the pancetta fat
and spread the mash inside it. Sprinkle with colby cheese and place under the

broiler for 4 minutes. Top with pancetta and chopped chives.

Per serving: Cal 312; Net Carbs 6g; Fat 25g; Protein 14g

Pancetta Wrapped Chicken Rolls

Ingredients for 4 servings

- 1 tbsp fresh chives, chopped
- 8 ounces blue cheese
- 1 lb chicken breasts, halved
- 12 pancetta slices
- 2 tomatoes, chopped
- Salt and black pepper, to taste

Instructions - Total Time: around 50 minutes

In a bowl, stir blue cheese, chives, tomatoes, pepper, and salt. Use a meat tenderizer to flatten the chicken breasts well, season with salt and pepper, and spread the cream cheese mixture on top. Roll them up and wrap in pancetta slices. Transfer to a greased baking dish and roast in the oven at 370 F for 30 minutes. Serve warm.

Per serving: Cal 623; Net Carbs 5g; Fat 48g; Protein 38g

Fish Taco Green Bowl with Red Cabbage

Ingredients for 4 servings

- 2 cups broccoli, riced
- 2 tsp ghee
- 4 tilapia fillets, cut into cubes
- ¼ tsp taco seasoning
- Salt and chili pepper to taste
- ¼ head red cabbage, shredded
- 1 ripe avocado, chopped
- 1 tsp dill

Instructions - Total Time: around 20 minutes

Sprinkle broccoli in a bowl with a little bit of water and microwave for 3

minutes. Fluff with a fork and set aside. Melt ghee in a skillet over medium

heat, rub the tilapia with taco seasoning, salt, dill, and chili and fry until

brown on all sides, 8 minutes in total; set aside. In 4 serving bowls, share the
broccoli, cabbage, fish, and avocado. Serve.

Per serving: Cal 269; Net Carbs 4g; Fat 23g; Protein 16.5g

Herbed Veal Rack

Ingredients for 4 servings

- ☐ 12 ounces veal rack
- ☐ 2 fennel bulbs, sliced
- ☐ Salt and black pepper to taste
- ☐ 3 tbsp olive oil
- ☐ ½ cup apple cider vinegar
- ☐ 1 tsp herbs de Provence

Instructions - Total Time: around 50 minutes

Preheat oven to 400 F. In a bowl, mix fennel with 2 tbsp of oil and vinegar,
toss to coat, and set to a baking dish. Season with herbs de Provence and bake
for 15 minutes.
Sprinkle pepper and salt on the veal, place into an greased pan over mediumhigh
heat, and cook for a couple of minutes. Place the veal in the baking dish
with the fennel, and bake for 20 minutes. Serve.

Cheese Scallops with Chorizo

Ingredients for 4 servings

- ☐ 2 tbsp ghee
- ☐ 16 fresh scallops
- ☐ 8 ounces chorizo, chopped
- ☐ 1 red bell pepper, sliced
- ☐ 1 cup red onions, chopped
- ☐ 1 cup Parmesan, grated

Instructions - Total Time: around 15 minutes

Melt the ghee in a skillet and cook onion and bell pepper for 5 minutes. Add in chorizo and stir-fry for another 3 minutes; set aside. Season scallops with salt and pepper. Sear the scallops in the same skillet for 2 minutes on each side. Add the chorizo mixture back and warm through. Transfer to a serving platter and top with Parmesan cheese.

Per serving: Cal 491; Net Carbs 5g; Fat 32g; Protein 36g

Chicken Ham & Turnip Pasta

Ingredients for 4 servings

- ☐ 6 slices chicken ham, chopped
- ☐ 1 lb turnips, spiralized
- ☐ 1 tbsp smoked paprika
- ☐ Salt and black pepper to taste
- ☐ 4 tbsp olive oil

Instructions - Total Time: around 30 minutes

Preheat oven to 450 F. Pour turnips into a bowl and add in paprika, salt, and

pepper; toss to coat. Spread the mixture on a greased baking sheet, scatter

ham on top, and drizzle with olive oil. Bake for 10 minutes until golden

brown.

Per serving: Cal 204; Net Carbs 1.6g; Fat 15g; Protein 10g

Kale & Mushroom Galette

Ingredients for 4 servings

- ☐ 1 tbsp flax seed powder
- ☐ 1 cup grated mozzarella
- ☐ 1 tbsp butter
- ☐ ½ cup almond flour
- ☐ ¼ cup coconut flour
- ☐ ½ tsp onion powder
- ☐ 1 tsp baking powder
- ☐ 3 oz cream cheese,
- ☐ 1 garlic clove, minced
- ☐ Salt and black pepper to taste
- ☐ 2/3 cup kale, chopped
- ☐ 2 oz mushrooms, sliced
- ☐ 1 oz grated Parmesan
- ☐ 2 tbsp olive oil for brushing

Instructions - Total Time: around 35 minutes

Preheat oven to 375 F. Line a baking sheet with parchment paper. In a bowl,

mix flax seed powder with 3 tbsp water and allow sitting for 5 minutes. Place
a pot over low heat, add in ½ cup mozzarella cheese and almond butter, and
melt both. Turn the heat off. Stir in almond and coconut flours, onion
powder, and baking powder. Pour in flax egg and combine until a quite sticky
dough forms. Transfer the dough to the sheet, cover with another parchment
paper and use a rolling pin to flatten into a circle. Remove parchment paper and spread cream cheese on the dough, leaving
about 2-inch border around the edges. Sprinkle with garlic, salt, and pepper.
Spread kale on top of the cheese, followed by mushrooms. Sprinkle the
remaining mozzarella and Parmesan cheeses on top. Fold the ends of the
crust over the filling and brush with olive oil. Bake for about 25-30 minutes.
Serve.

Braised Sage-Flavored Lamb Chops

Ingredients for 6 servings

- ☐ 6 lamb chops
- ☐ 1 tbsp sage
- ☐ 1 tsp thyme
- ☐ 1 onion, sliced
- ☐ 3 garlic cloves, minced
- ☐ 2 tbsp olive oil
- ☐ ½ cup white wine
- ☐ Salt and black pepper to taste

Instructions - Total Time: around 1 hour 25 minutes

Heat the olive oil in a pan. Add onion and garlic and cook for 3 minutes, until

soft; set aside. Rub sage and thyme onto the lamb and sear it in the pan for 3

minutes per side; reserve. Deglaze the pan with white wine and pour in 1 cup of water. Bring the mixture to a boil. Cook until the liquid reduces by half.

Add the lamb, lower the heat, and let simmer for 1 hour. Serve warm.

Per serving: Cal 397; Net Carbs 4.3g; Fat 30g; Protein 16g

Turnip Chips with Avocado Dip

Ingredients for 6 servings

- ☐ 2 avocados, mashed
- ☐ 2 tsp lime juice
- ☐ 2 garlic cloves, minced
- ☐ 2 tbsp olive oil
- ☐ For turnip chips
- ☐ 1 ½ pounds turnips, sliced
- ☐ 1 tbsp olive oil
- ☐ Salt to taste
- ☐ ½ tsp garlic powder

Instructions - Total Time: around 20 minutes

Stir avocado in lime juice, 2 tbsp of olive oil, and garlic until well combined.

Remove to a bowl. Preheat oven to 300 F. Set turnip slices on a greased

baking sheet; toss with garlic powder, 1 tbsp of olive oil, and salt. Bake for

15 minutes. Serve with chilled avocado dip.

Per serving: Cal 269; Net Carbs: 9g; Fat: 27g; Protein: 3g

SNACK & SIDES

Jalapeño Nacho Wings

Ingredients for 4 servings

- ☐ 2 cups shredded Mexican cheese blend
- ☐ 16 chicken wings, halved
- ☐ ½ cup butter, melted
- ☐ 1 cup golden flaxseed meal
- ☐ 2 tbsp chopped green chilies
- ☐ 1 cup chopped scallions
- ☐ 1 jalapeño pepper, sliced

Instructions - Total Time: around 45 minutes

Preheat oven to 350 F. Brush the chicken with butter. Spread the flaxseed meal on a wide plate and roll in each chicken wing. Place on a baking sheet and bake for 30-35 minutes or until golden brown and cooked within.

Sprinkle with the cheese blend, green chilies, scallions, and jalapeño pepper on top. Serve immediately.

Cheesy Bacon & Eggplant Gratin

Ingredients for 4 servings

- ☐ 6 bacon slices, chopped
- ☐ 3 large eggplants, sliced
- ☐ 1 tbsp dried oregano
- ☐ 2 tbsp chopped parsley
- ☐ Salt and black pepper to taste
- ☐ ½ cup crumbled feta cheese
- ☐ ¾ cup heavy cream
- ☐ ½ cup shredded Parmesan

Instructions - Total Time: around 50 minutes

Preheat oven to 400 F. Put bacon in a skillet and fry over medium heat until
brown and crispy, 6 minutes; transfer to a plate. Arrange half of eggplants in
a greased baking sheet and season with oregano, parsley, salt, and pepper.
Scatter half of bacon and half of feta cheese on top and repeat the layering

process using the remaining ingredients. In a bowl, combine heavy cream with half of the Parmesan cheese, and spread on top of the layered ingredients. Sprinkle with the remaining Parmesan. Bake until the cream is bubbly and the gratin golden, 20 minutes. Serve.

Per serving: Cal 433; Net Carbs 1.7g; Fat 29g; Protein 16g

Wrapped Halloumi in Bacon

Ingredients for 4 servings

- ½ lb halloumi cheese, cut into 16 cubes
- 16 bacon strips
- ½ cup swerve brown sugar
- ½ cup mayonnaise
- ¼ cup hot sauce

Instructions - Total Time: around 30 minutes

Lay bacon in a skillet and cook over medium heat on both sides until crisp, 5 minutes; transfer to a plate. Wrap each halloumi cheese with a bacon strip and secure with a toothpick each. Place on a baking sheet. In a bowl, combine swerve brown sugar, mayonnaise, and hot sauce. Pour the mixture all over the bacon-halloumi pieces and bake in the oven at 350 F for 10 minutes. Serve chilled.

Sweet Mustard Mini Sausages

Ingredients for 4 servings

- ☐ 1 cup swerve brown sugar
- ☐ 3 tbsp almond flour
- ☐ 2 tsp mustard powder
- ☐ ¼ cup lemon juice
- ☐ ¼ cup white wine vinegar
- ☐ 1 tsp tamari sauce
- ☐ 2 lb mini smoked sausages

Instructions - Total Time: around 15 minutes

In a pot, combine swerve brown sugar, almond flour, and mustard. Gradually
stir in lemon juice, vinegar, and tamari sauce. Bring to a boil over medium
heat while stirring until thickened, 2 minutes. Mix in sausages until properly
coated. Cook them for 5 minutes. Serve warm.

Per serving: Cal 744; Net Carbs 7.2g; Fat 45g; Protein 24g

Chili Broccoli & Pancetta Roast

Ingredients for 4 servings

- 1 lb broccoli rabe, halved
- 6 pancetta slices, chopped
- 2 tbsp olive oil
- ¼ tsp red chili flakes

Instructions - Total Time: around 40 minutes

Preheat oven to 425 F. Place broccoli rabe in a greased baking sheet and top
with pancetta. Drizzle with olive oil, season to taste, and sprinkle with chili
flakes. Roast for 30 minutes. Serve warm and enjoy!

Per serving: Cal 125; Net Carbs 0.2g; Fat 10g; Protein 7g

Chili Turnip Fries

Ingredients for 4 servings

- ☐ 4 large parsnips, sliced
- ☐ 3 tbsp ground pork rinds
- ☐ 3 tbsp olive oil
- ☐ ¼ tsp red chili flakes

Instructions - Total Time: around 50 minutes

Preheat oven to 425 F. Pour parsnips into a bowl and add in the pork rinds.

Toss and place the parsnips a baking sheet. Drizzle with olive oil and sprinkle

with chili flakes. Bake until crispy, 40-45 minutes, tossing halfway. Serve.

Per serving: Cal 260; Net Carbs 22.6g; Fat 11g; Protein 3g

Buttery Radish & Minute Steak Sauté

Ingredients for 4 servings

- ☐ 10 oz minute steak, cut into small pieces
- ☐ 3 tbsp butter
- ☐ 1½ lb radishes, quartered
- ☐ 1 garlic clove, minced
- ☐ 2 tbsp freshly chopped thyme

Instructions - Total Time: around 30 minutes

Melt butter in a skillet over medium heat, season the meat with salt and

pepper, and brown it until brown on all sides, 12 minutes; transfer to a plate.

Add and sauté radishes, garlic, and thyme until the radishes are cooked, 10

minutes. Plate and serve warm.

Per serving: Cal 252; Net Carbs 0.4g; Fat 16g; Protein 21g

Cheddar Bacon & Celeriac Bake

Ingredients for 4 servings

- 6 bacon slices, chopped
- 3 tbsp butter
- 3 garlic cloves, minced
- 3 tbsp almond flour
- 2 cups coconut cream
- 1 cup chicken broth
- Salt and black pepper to taste
- 1 lb celeriac, peeled and sliced
- 2 cups shredded cheddar
- ¼ cup chopped scallions

Instructions - Total Time: around 50 minutes

Preheat oven to 400 F. Add bacon to a skillet and fry over medium heat until

brown and crispy. Spoon onto a plate. Melt butter in the same skillet and

sauté garlic for 1 minute. Mix in almond flour and cook for another minute.

Whisk in coconut cream, chicken broth, salt, and pepper. Simmer for 5 minutes. Spread a layer of the sauce in a greased casserole dish and arrange a layer celeriac on top. Cover with more sauce, top with some bacon and cheddar cheese, and scatter scallions on top. Repeat the layering process until the ingredients are exhausted. Bake for 35 minutes. Let rest for a few minutes and serve.

Per serving: Cal 981; Net Carbs 20g; Fat 86g; Protein 28g

Chicken Ham with Mini Bell Peppers

Ingredients for 4 servings

- 12 mini green bell peppers, halved and deseeded
- 4 slices chicken ham, chopped
- 1 tbsp chopped parsley
- 8 oz cream cheese
- ½ tbsp hot sauce
- 2 tbsp melted butter
- 1 cup shredded Gruyere

Instructions - Total Time: around 30 minutes

Preheat oven to 400 F. Place peppers in a greased baking dish and set aside.

In a bowl, combine chicken ham, parsley, cream cheese, hot sauce, and

butter. Spoon the mixture into the peppers and sprinkle Gruyere cheese on top. Bake until the cheese melts, about 20 minutes. Serve.

Per serving: Cal 408; Net Carbs 4g; Fat 32g; Protein 19g

Crispy Baked Cheese Asparagus

Ingredients for 4 servings

- ☐ 1 cup grated Pecorino Romano cheese
- ☐ 4 slices Serrano ham, chopped
- ☐ 2 lb asparagus, stalks trimmed
- ☐ ¾ cup coconut cream
- ☐ 3 garlic cloves, minced
- ☐ 1 cup crushed pork rinds
- ☐ 1 cup grated mozzarella
- ☐ ½ tsp sweet paprika

Instructions - Total Time: around 40 minutes

Preheat oven to 400 F. Arrange asparagus on a greased baking dish and pour
coconut cream on top. Scatter the garlic, serrano ham, and pork rinds on top
and sprinkle with Pecorino cheese, mozzarella cheese, and paprika. Bake
until the cheese melts and is golden and asparagus tender, 30 minutes. Serve
warm.

Easy Bacon & Cheese Balls

Ingredients for 4 servings

- ☐ 7 bacon slices
- ☐ 6 oz cream cheese
- ☐ 6 oz shredded Gruyere cheese
- ☐ 2 tbsp butter, softened
- ☐ ½ tsp red chili flakes

Instructions - Total Time: around 30 minutes

Put bacon in a skillet and fry over medium heat until crispy, 5 minutes.

Transfer to a plate to cool and cruble it. Pour the bacon grease into a bowl
and mix in cream cheese, Gruyere cheese, butter, and red chili flakes.

Refrigerate to set for 15 minutes. Remove and mold into walnut-sized balls.

Roll in the crumbled bacon. Plate and serve.

Per serving: Cal 538; Net Carbs 0.5g; Fat 50g; Protein 22g

DESSERTS

Lemon-Yogurt Mousse

Ingredients for 4 servings

- ☐ 24 oz plain yogurt, strained overnight in a cheesecloth
- ☐ 2 cups swerve confectioner's sugar
- ☐ 2 lemons, juiced and zested
- ☐ 1 cup whipped cream + extra for garnish

Instructions - Total Time: around 5 min + cooling time

Whip the plain yogurt in a bowl with a hand mixer until light and fluffy. Mix
in the swerve sugar, lemon juice, and salt. Fold in the whipped cream to
combine. Spoon the mousse into serving cups and refrigerate for 1 hour.
Swirl with extra whipped cream and garnish with lemon zest.

Per serving: Cal 223; Net Carbs 3g; Fat 18g; Protein 12g

Strawberry Chocolate Mousse

Ingredients for 4 servings

- ☐ 1 cup fresh strawberries, sliced
- ☐ 3 eggs
- ☐ 1 cup dark chocolate chips
- ☐ 1 cup heavy cream
- ☐ 1 vanilla extract
- ☐ 1 tbsp swerve sugar

Instructions - Total Time: around 30 minutes

Melt the chocolate in a microwave-safe bowl in the microwave oven for 1

minute; let cool for 8 minutes. In a bowl, whip the heavy cream until very

soft. Whisk in the eggs, vanilla extract, and swerve sugar. Fold in the cooled

chocolate. Divide the mousse between glasses, top with the strawberry and

chill in the fridge. Serve.

Per serving: Cal 400; Net Carbs 1.7g; Fat 25g; Protein 8g

Maple Lemon Cake

Ingredients for 4 servings

- ☐ 4 eggs
- ☐ 1 cup sour cream
- ☐ 2 lemons, zested and juiced
- ☐ 1 tsp vanilla extract
- ☐ 2 cups almond flour
- ☐ 2 tbsp coconut flour
- ☐ 2 tsp baking powder
- ☐ ½ cup xylitol
- ☐ 1 tsp cardamom powder
- ☐ ½ tsp ground ginger
- ☐ A pinch of salt
- ☐ ¼ cup maple syrup

Instructions - Total Time: around 30 minutes

Preheat oven to 400 F. Grease a cake pan with melted butter. In a bowl, beat
eggs, sour cream, lemon juice, and vanilla extract until smooth. In another

bowl, whisk almond and coconut flours, baking powder, xylitol, cardamom, ginger, salt, lemon zest, and half of maple syrup. Combine both mixtures until smooth and pour the batter into the pan. Bake for 25 minutes or until a toothpick inserted comes out clean. Transfer to a wire rack, let cool, and drizzle with the remaining maple syrup. Serve sliced.

Per serving: Cal 441; Net Carbs 8.5g; Fat 29g; Protein 33g

Saffron & Cardamom Coconut Bars

Ingredients for 4 servings

- ☐ 3 ½ ounces ghee
- ☐ 10 saffron threads
- ☐ 1 ⅓ cups coconut milk
- ☐ 1 ¾ cups shredded coconut
- ☐ 4 tbsp sweetener
- ☐ 1 tsp cardamom powder

Instructions - Total Time: around 15 min + chilling time

Combine the shredded coconut with 1 cup of coconut milk. In another bowl,
mix the remaining coconut milk with the sweetener and saffron. Let sit for 30
minutes, and then combine the two mixtures. Heat the ghee in a wok. Add in
the mixture and cook for 5 minutes on low heat, stirring continuously. Mix in

cardamom and cook for 5 more minutes. Spread the mixture onto a greased
baking pan. Freeze for 2 hours. Cut into bars and serve.

Per serving: Cal 130; Net Carbs 1.4g; Fat 12g; Protein 2g

Granny Smith Apple Tart

Ingredients for 6 servings

- ☐ 2 cups almond flour
- ☐ ¼ cup + 6 tbsp butter
- ☐ 1 ¼ tsp cinnamon
- ☐ 1 cup sweetener
- ☐ 2 cups sliced Granny Smith
- ☐ ½ tsp lemon juice

Instructions - Total Time: around 45 minutes

Preheat oven to 375 F. Combine 6 tbsp of butter, almond flour, 1 tsp of cinnamon, and ⅓ cup of sweetener in a bowl. Press this mixture into a greased pan. Bake for 5 minutes. Combine apples and lemon juice in a bowl and arrange them on top of the crust. Combine the remaining butter and sweetener and brush over the apples. Bake for 30 minutes. Dust with remaining cinnamon and serve.

Chocolate Mocha Ice Bombs

Ingredients for 4 servings

- ½ pound cream cheese
- 4 tbsp powdered sweetener
- 2 ounces strong coffee
- 2 tbsp cocoa powder
- 1 ounce cocoa butter, melted
- 2 ½ oz dark chocolate, melted

Instructions - Total Time: around 10 min + chilling time

Combine cream cheese, sweetener, coffee, and cocoa powder in a food processor. Roll 2 tbsp of the mixture and place on a lined tray. Mix the melted cocoa butter and chocolate and coat the bombs with it. Freeze for 2 hours.

Per serving: Cal 127; Net Carbs 1.4g; Fat 13g; Protein 2g

Almond & Coconut Bark

Ingredients for 8 servings

- ½ cup almonds
- ½ cup coconut butter
- 10 drops stevia
- ¼ tsp salt
- ½ cup coconut flakes
- 4 ounces dark chocolate

Instructions - Total Time: around 15 min + chilling time

Preheat oven to 350 F. Place almonds in a baking sheet and toast for 5 minutes. Melt together the butter and chocolate. Stir in stevia. Line a cookie sheet with waxed paper and spread the chocolate evenly. Scatter the almonds on top and sprinkle with salt. Refrigerated for 1 hour. Serve.

Per serving: Cal 161; Net Carbs 1.9g; Fat 15g; Protein 2g

Coconut Butter Ice Cream

Ingredients for 4 servings

- ½ cup smooth coconut butter
- ½ cup swerve sugar
- 3 cups half and half
- 1 tsp vanilla extract

Instructions - Total Time: around 10 min + freezing time

Beat coconut butter and swerve sugar in a bowl with a hand mixer until

smooth. Gradually whisk in half and half until thoroughly combined. Mix in

vanilla. Pour the mixture into a loaf pan and freeze for 45 minutes until

firmed up. Scoop into glasses when ready to eat and serve.

Per serving: Cal 290; Net Carbs 6g; Fat 23g; Protein 13g

Chia Pudding

Ingredients for 4 servings

- ☐ 4 tbsp chia seeds
- ☐ ½ cup almond milk
- ☐ 1 cup coconut cream
- ☐ ½ cup sour cream
- ☐ ½ tsp vanilla extract
- ☐ ¼ tsp cardamon powder
- ☐ 1 tbsp stevia

Instructions - Total Time: around 20 min + cooling time

Add all the ingredients in a mixing bowl and stir to combine. Leave to rest
for 20 minutes. Apportion the mixture among bowls. Serve and enjoy!

Per serving: Cal 258; Net Carbs: 2g; Fat: 24g; Protein: 5g

Mom's Walnut Cookies

Ingredients for 12 servings

- ☐ 1 egg
- ☐ 2 cups ground pecans
- ☐ ¼ cup sweetener
- ☐ ½ tsp baking soda
- ☐ 1 tbsp ghee
- ☐ 20 walnuts, chopped

Instructions - Total Time: around 25 minutes

Preheat oven to 350 F. In a bowl, mix all the ingredients, except for walnuts,
until combined. Make balls out of the mixture and press them with your
thumb onto a lined cookie sheet. Top with walnuts. Bake for 12 minutes.

Per serving: Cal 101; Net Carbs: 1g; Fat: 11g; Protein: 2g

Almond Ice Cream

Ingredients for 4 servings

- 2 cups heavy cream
- 1 tbsp xylitol
- ½ cup smooth almond butter
- 1 tbsp olive oil
- 1 tbsp vanilla extract
- ½ tsp salt
- 2 egg yolks
- ½ cup almonds, chopped
- ½ cup swerve sugar

Instructions - Total Time: around 40 min + cooling time

Warm heavy cream with almond butter, olive oil, xylitol, and salt in a small
pan over low heat without boiling, for 3 minutes. Beat the egg yolks until
creamy in color. Stir the eggs into the cream mixture. Refrigerate cream
mixture for 30 minutes. Remove and stir in swerve sugar. Pour mixture into

ice cream machine and churn it according to the manufacturer's instructions.

Stir in almonds and spoon mixture into loaf pan. Refrigerate for at least for 2 hours.

Per serving: Cal 552; Net Carbs 6.2g; Fat 45.4g; Protein 9g